WHAT DOES A MAIL CARRIER DO?

What Does a Community Helper Do?

Lisa Trumbauer

Words to Know

address (ah-DRESS)—The name of a person, street, town, state, and zip code on a letter that tells mail carriers who gets the letter. Also, to write down directions for delivery.

deliver (duh-LIV-ur)—To bring mail from the post office to a person's home.

route (root)—A regular way of traveling. A mail carrier travels the same way everyday.

sort (sort)—To put the mail together in a certain way.

worker (WER-kur)—A person who does a job.

ZIP code (zip kohd)—A number of five digits that tells mail carriers where a letter is going.

Enslow Elementary

an imprint of

 Enslow Publishers, Inc.

40 Industrial Road
Box 398
Berkeley Heights, NJ 07922
USA

PO Box 38
Aldershot
Hants GU12 6BP
UK

http://www.enslow.com

Contents

You can mail a card to a friend.

Making a Card

It is a special day. You made a card, but your friend lives in another town. How can you get the card to your friend? You can mail it!

ahn
PO ___ 52
Dexter, Maine 04930

Betsy Rossi
12 Main Street
Town, State 12345

Address

ZIP code

Make sure the envelope has an address and a ZIP code.

This worker sorts mail at the post office.

Going to the Mailbox

Put your card in the mailbox. A mail carrier will pick up your card. The mail carrier will take it to the post office. Workers there will sort the mail by ZIP code. Every town has a ZIP code. This number tells the workers where the mail goes.

Where Does Mail Go?

Your card goes to the post office near where your friend lives. A worker there sorts the mail by streets. Then the mail carrier delivers the card.

Mail carriers pick up mail at mailboxes.

Every Town Has a Mail Carrier

Every town has at least one mail carrier. A big city has many. Some mail carriers empty mailboxes. They take the mail to the post office. Other mail carriers carry heavy bags. Their bags are full of mail. They walk with their bags to deliver the mail.

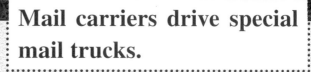

Mail carriers drive special mail trucks.

What Does a Mail Carrier Drive?

In smaller towns, mail carriers might drive a mail truck. They load the mail into the truck. Then they drive from home to home. They drive to stores and businesses, too. They put the mail in mailboxes.

This mail carrier drives his own car to deliver mail.

Towns in the country may only have one mail carrier. The mail carrier might drive a mail truck. Or the mail carrier might drive his or her own car.

Mail carriers deliver mail in all kinds of weather.

When Do Mail Carriers Work?

Mail carriers work almost every day. They deliver the mail on sunny days and rainy days. They deliver the mail on snowy days.

Mail carriers know towns well.

Mail Carriers and Their Towns

Mail carriers must know their town very well. They drive the same route every day. They know the names of the streets. They know the names of many people on their routes.

Mail carriers deliver mail to many people and places.

Delivering the Mail

Mail carriers around the world help people. They deliver letters and packages. They also deliver newspapers and catalogs. They even deliver birthday cards!

How to Address an Envelope

Would you like to send a letter to your friend? You will need to know how to address an envelope. An address helps mail carriers deliver mail to the right person.

You will need:
- your friend's address
- your address
- a piece of paper, 8-1/2 x 11 inches
- an envelope
- a stamp
- a pencil or pen

On the piece of paper:
1. Write a letter to your friend.

2. Fold it neatly so it fits inside the envelope.

3. Be sure to seal the envelope.

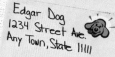

On the envelope:
Hint: Write in pencil first. If you make a mistake you can erase it and then fix it. You can go over the pencil with a pen.
1. Write your friend's name in the center of the envelope. Be sure to write their first name and last name.

2. Write the street your friend lives on under the name.

3. Write the city, state, and ZIP code under the street.

4. In the top left corner, write your name and address.

5. Ask the adults you live with for a stamp.

6. Place the stamp in the top right corner of the envelope.

Now you can write letters and mail them to your friends and family!

Learn More

Books

Flanagan, Alice K. *Here Comes Mr. Eventoff with the Mail!* New York: Children's Press, 1998.

Flanagan, Alice K. *Letter Carriers.* Minneapolis, Minn.: Compass Point Books, 2000.

Macken, JoAnn Early. *Mail Carrier.* Milwaukee, Wisc.: Weekly Reader Early Learning Library, 2003.

Stewart, Alex. *Sending a Letter.* New York: Franklin Watts, 1999.

Internet Addresses

National Postal Museum: Activity Zone
<http://www.postalmuseum.si.edu/>
 Click on Activity Zone to find fun stuff to do.

United States Postal Service
<http://www.usps.com/>
 Find a ZIP code and check out new stamps at this site.

Index

Note to Teachers and Parents: The *What Does a Community Helper Do?* series supports curriculum standards for K–4 learning about community services and helpers. The Words to Know section introduces subject-specific vocabulary. Early readers may require help with these new words.

Series Literacy Consultant:

Allan A. De Fina, Ph.D.
Past President of the New Jersey Reading Association
Professor, Department of Literacy Education
New Jersey City University

Enslow Elementary, an imprint of Enslow Publishers, Inc.

Enslow Elementary® is a registered trademark of Enslow Publishers, Inc.

Copyright © 2005 by Enslow Publishers, Inc.

Library of Congress Cataloging-in-Publication Data

Trumbauer, Lisa, 1963-
    What does a mail carrier do? / Lisa Trumbauer.
      p. cm. — (What does a community helper do?)
    Includes bibliographical references and index.
    ISBN 0-7660-2544-6
    1. Letter carriers—Juvenile literature. I. Title. II. Series.
HE6241.T78 2005
383'.145—dc22   2004006893

Printed in the United States of America

10 9 8 7 6 5 4 3 2 1

To Our Readers:

We have done our best to make sure all Internet Addresses in this book were active and appropriate when we went to press. However, the author and the publisher have no control over and assume no liability for the material available on those Internet sites or on other Web sites they may link to. Any comments or suggestions can be sent by e-mail to comments@enslow.com or to the address on the back cover.

Illustration Credits: Associated Press, p. 10; Associated Press, Salina Journal, p. 16; Associated Press, Telegraph Herald, p. 14; Corel Corporation, p. 1 (tree background); Enslow Publishers, Inc., p. 22; Hemera Technologies, Inc. 1997-2000, pp. 2, 15, 20; Dwight Kuhn, p. 6; Lawrence Migdale, pp. 4, 12; Photri/Macdonald, p. 18; Punchstock, p. 1 (mail carrier); Star Ledger photo by Warren S. Westura, p. 8.

Cover Illustration: Punchstock (mail carrier), Corel Corporation (tree background); top left to right (Associated Press; Lawrence Migdale; Associated Press, Telegraph Herald; Photri/Macdonald.).